DEDICATION

To my beautiful bride, Melissa "Bo"

Who has walked beside me since we were just a couple of high school kids with big dreams. You've been my anchor, my encourager, my home — and you are "my person." Through every high and low, especially the valleys we never saw coming, your faith and fierce love never wavered.

This wouldn't exist without you. And someday, when we've turned the last page and closed the last deal, it's you and me doing this together — free and clear, just like we've always talked about. That's the plan, and I know you are holding me to it.

To our twelve amazing children and our growing tribe of grandbabies.

You are my legacy and my greatest joy. Every mortgage I've ever closed, every page I've ever written — it's always been for you. I hope you inherit a world where the financial industry is a little more honest than the one I walked into. And if it's not, at least you'll have the book.

And to the One who's carried us through it all — Jesus.

This is for Your glory. Everything good in my life has come from Your hand. The faith that held us in the valleys. The grace that met us in the mornings. None of this makes sense without You in the middle of it.

Family, faith, and a whole lotta grit — that's what built this.

Before We Start

If you read *Unlocked*, you already know the problem. You've seen page five. You know what $510,000 in interest looks like at the bottom of a $400,000 loan, and you know the industry has been counting on you not reading that far. You didn't pick up this book to hear the problem again.

This is the book with the answer.

If you haven't read *Unlocked*, that's fine — everything you need is right here. The Introduction will catch you up. Then we're going to show you a different way to carry a mortgage, one that's built around your cash flow instead of the bank's calendar, and what it looks like when a $400,000 debt is gone in six years instead of thirty.

Start with the Introduction. I'll be at the kitchen table.

Table of Contents

KEEP THE CASH™

MORTGAGE

THE COMPLETE GUIDE TO PAYING OFF
YOUR MORTGAGE IN YEARS – NOT DECADES

**YOUR MORTGAGE WAS DESIGNED TO
MAKE THE BANK RICH. HERE'S
HOW YOU GET RICH INSTEAD.**

MICHAEL DENDY

"I HAVE 12 KIDS…I HAVE TO CLOSE LOANS!"

MI-1632270 | Edge Home Finance Corporation supports Equal Housing Opportunity.

NMLS ID# 891464 (www.nmlsconsumeraccess.org). Interest rates and products are subject to change without notice and may or may not be available at the time of loan commitment or lock in. Borrowers must qualify at closing for all benefits. This is not an offer to lend and each borrower must qualify on their own merits to purchase a home.

THIS PAGE IS INTENTIONALLY LEFT BLANK.

I'VE ALWAYS WANTED TO BE ABLE TO SAY THAT.

I'VE ALWAYS WANTED TO LET CONSUMERS KNOW THAT THIS IS SUCH A WASTE OF PAPER, JUST LIKE THE PAGE THAT IS LEFT BLANK ON YOUR BANK STATEMENT.

IT'S STUPID

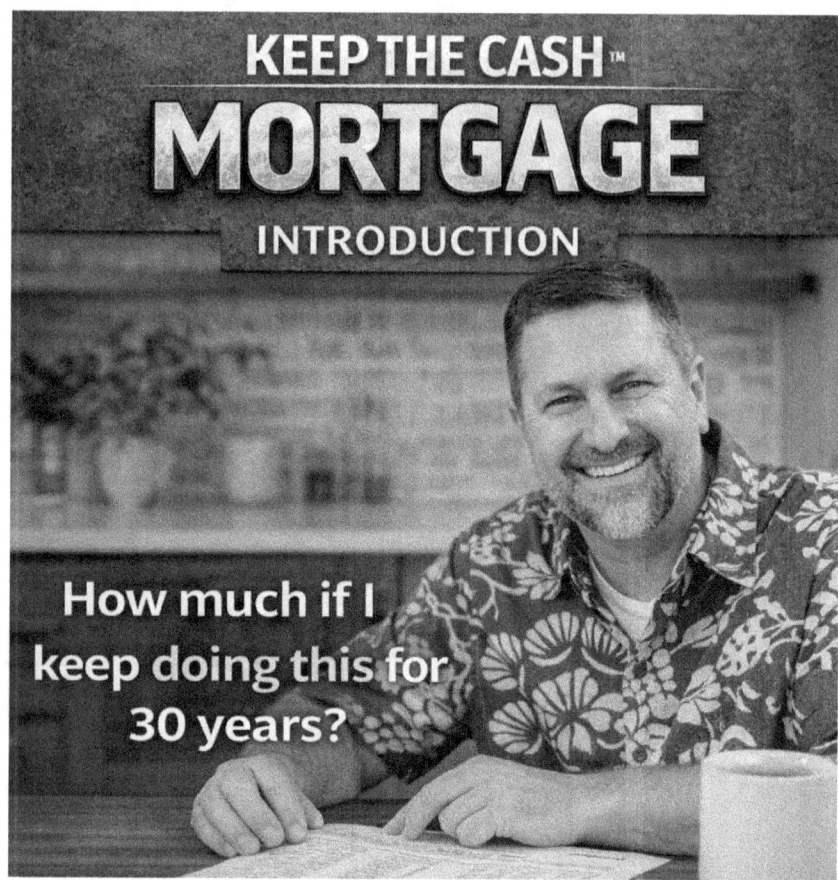

KEEP THE CASH™
MORTGAGE
INTRODUCTION

How much if I keep doing this for 30 years?

INTRODUCTION

The Most Expensive Checking Account in America

I was sitting at my kitchen table, our kitchen table, the one Bo had her dad build, the one that has survived twelve kids and approximately 27,000 meals, paint, stains and at least one incident involving a sharpie that we don't talk about. I had a piece of paper in front of me that I wished I'd never pulled up. It was my own amortization schedule. Not a client's. Mine.

I've been in the mortgage business long enough and have closed hundreds of loans. When I started in this business, I went and took the licensing exam and I passed. I didn't know a whole lot. I mean, I knew what a mortgage was. But Fannie Mae and Freddie Mac? I thought they were a married couple. Turns out they're government-sponsored enterprises. Which is basically the same thing, except the government doesn't bring a casserole to your closing. I've sat across from more families than I can count and walked them through the paperwork, explained the numbers, answered the questions. I knew how amortization worked. I'd explained it a hundred times.

But I had never actually sat down and run the full thirty-year projection on my own house. My own balance. My own rate. Every row, all the way to the bottom. So I did. And then I just sat there for a minute.

The number at the bottom of the interest column, the total I was on track to pay the bank in interest, if I just kept doing what everybody told me to do, made my payment every month, and finished the loan like a responsible adult, was just over $387,000. I borrowed $310,000.

I was going to give the bank $387,000 just in interest. Before a single dollar of that touched the actual balance I owed. Before a single dollar went toward the house. Just the cost of borrowing. Just the meter running for thirty years while I went to work and made my payment and felt good about myself for not being late.

My coffee had gotten cold by the time I looked up from that paper. I didn't notice.

Here's what made it worse. I went back and looked at year one. Twelve payments. Twelve months of doing everything right. Of every dollar I sent to the bank that year, 85 cents went straight to interest. Fifteen cents went to the balance I actually owed. I could have worked the whole first year for free, just handed the bank a check for twelve months of payments and barely moved the needle on what I owed.

That's not a mistake. That's not a glitch in the system. That is the system, working exactly the way it was designed to work.

I've got twelve kids. I don't say that for sympathy. I say it because when I looked at that number...$387,000 in interest over thirty years, I didn't think about it in abstract terms. I thought about what $387,000 means to a family that is always, always, always figuring out how to make the money work. I thought about college. I thought about weddings. I thought about the years when two kids needed braces at the same time and we just kind of held our breath and figured it out. I thought about every month where there wasn't a whole lot of cushion, and how the bank was collecting $70 a day from me whether there was cushion or not.

And then the question landed. The one I couldn't shake.

What if I didn't have to?

Not "what if I paid a little extra every month" I'd tried that math and it helped, but it wasn't the answer. Not "what if I refinanced into a 15-year", I have done that before. I knew what that did to the monthly payment, and with twelve mouths at the table that conversation had a short shelf life. Something different. Something structural. What if the whole machine could be rebuilt? What if there was a way to take the income I was already earning, income that already dwarfed my mortgage balance if you added it up over thirty years, and put it to work against that balance every single day instead of letting it sit in a checking account that had no idea a mortgage existed? What if I could find a way to reverse engineer a loan the way that credit card companies charge interest? That question is why this book exists.

By the time you get to the end of it, you're going to have your own number. Not mine. Yours. Your balance, your rate, your income, your specific projection of what the bank is on track to collect from you between now and the day you make that last payment. And right next to it, you're going to have a different number, what that same mortgage looks like when you change the architecture underneath it.

The gap between those two numbers is what this is about. That gap is real. It's sitting there right now, whether you're looking at it or not.

I'd rather you look at it.

PART ONE:

THE PROBLEM WITH YOUR PAYCHECK

The 30-Year Mortgage Is Draining Your Paycheck

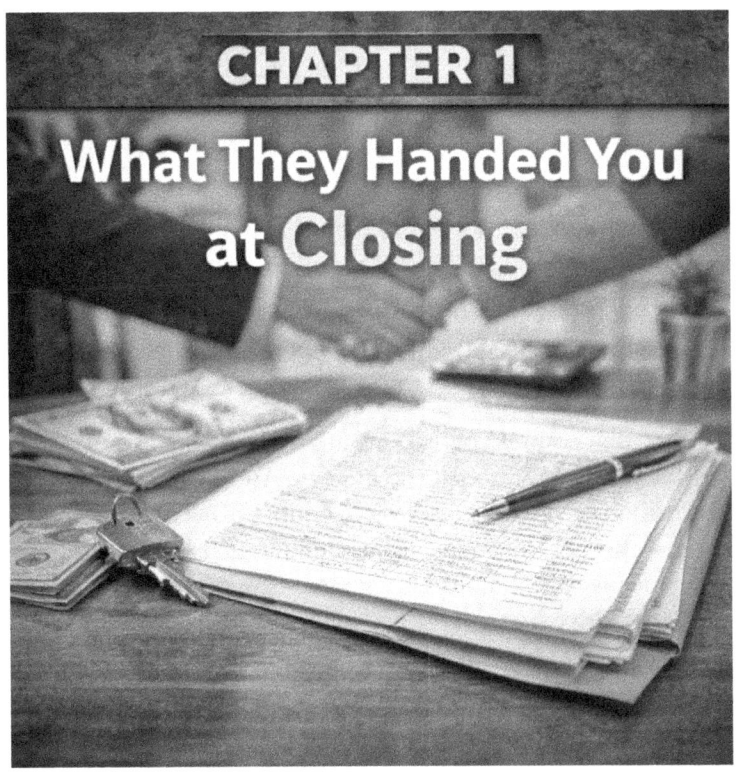

CHAPTER 1

What They Handed You at Closing

(And What They Didn't)

I remember the table.

It was one of those big fake-mahogany conference tables that every title company in America seems to own. The kind that's supposed to make the whole thing feel serious and official. There was a notary with a practiced smile, a stack of papers thick enough to have its own gravity, and a nice pen handed over with a little flourish. Why? Because you're about to sign your name so many times the pen starts to feel like part of your hand.

They walked you through it. Sort of. They'd point to a line and say sign here, flip to another page and say initial here... I once counted the number of times a borrower signed their name at a closing. I lost count around forty-seven. By the end, they weren't even reading it. They were just signing. You could have slipped in a page that said "I agree to name my firstborn after the title company" and they'd have initialed it without blinking. I know. Because I've been on both sides of that table and somewhere in the middle you just started signing because that's what you do at a closing table. You trust the process.

When it was over, they shook your hand, congratulated you, maybe took a picture. You walked out with a set of keys and that enormous warm feeling that you'd done it.

What you didn't walk out with was the truth about what you'd just signed.

I know that sounds dramatic. But I've been at the table. I've handed the pen. I've watched the ink dry. And I can tell you that in all the closings I have been to, I have almost never seen a borrower walk out of that room actually understanding what that number on page five means. We smile, we shake hands, we congratulate them, and then they drive home with keys and a payment and a number nobody explained. Not some hidden trap buried in the fine print. One specific number. Right there on the page, legally disclosed. And unless somebody stopped and explained what it actually meant, which almost nobody ever does, you signed right past it. I'm sorry in advance.

The Number on Page Five

Every mortgage comes with a federal Closing Disclosure. On page five, in a section labeled **Loan Calculations**, there's a line that reads: ***Total of Payments***. That's the total dollar amount you will pay the bank over the entire life of the loan — every payment, first to last, thirty years from now.

Go find yours right now if you have it. Page five. That number. Sit with it.

Because here's what it's telling you: how much the bank is going to make off your family over the next three decades. How much of what you earn will flow out of your checking account and into a financial institution that is counting on you to make your payment every month, not ask too many questions, and never think too hard about whether there's a better way.

THE MATH THEY HOPED YOU'D SKIP	$400,000 @ 6.5% / 30 Years
Monthly payment (principal + interest)	**$2,528**
Total of all payments over 30 years	**$910,178**
Amount you actually borrowed	**$400,000**
Total interest paid to the bank	**$510,178**
Year 1 — of your $30,336 in payments:	
→ Went to your principal balance	$4,471
→ Went to the bank as interest	**$25,868**

That last line. In year one, 85 cents of every dollar you pay goes straight to interest. You get 15 cents. For the first twelve months of your loan, you are mostly working for the bank, a little bit for yourself. Every single month.

That's not a flaw in the system. That's the feature.

How the Schedule Is Built

Here's something they don't teach you at the closing table. Or in school. Or anywhere, really. When I first explained amortization to my oldest kid, he looked at me and said "Dad, that's basically stealing." I said son, it's not stealing. It's just the rules. He said what's the difference. I didn't have a great answer for that. The 30-year amortization schedule is specifically structured so that the bank's profit — interest — gets collected first. It's called front-loading. The bank knows that money paid early is worth more, because they get to put it to work longer. Here's what that looks like over the life of that $400,000 loan:

Year	Annual Paid	→ Principal	→ Interest	Balance Left
1	$30,336	$4,471	$25,868	$395,529
10	$30,339	$8,012	$22,326	$339,104
20	$30,339	$15,321	$15,018	$222,661
30	$30,339	$29,297	$1,042	$0

Year twenty. You've made twenty years of payments — $303,360 handed to the bank. Your remaining balance: $222,661. You still owe over half of what you originally borrowed after twenty years of faithfully paying every month. That isn't an accident. It was all disclosed. On page five.

Does the cost have to be that high?

The answer is no. And the rest of this book is the proof.

Disclosed. But Never Explained.

The Total of Payments line is legally required on every U.S. mortgage closing documents. Every single person who's signed mortgage papers in the last fifty-plus years has technically been told what their loan was going to cost them. Over the past 10 years, the documents have made it extremely obvious. The problem is that they are buried on the back pages. Homeowners just weren't taught what it meant.

The law requires disclosure. It does not require education. There's a canyon between those two things, and the mortgage industry has been parking its profits in that canyon for decades. You were told. You just weren't helped to understand. And in the

16

mortgage business, that gap is worth hundreds of billions of dollars a year.

The 30-year mortgage is not a law of physics. It's not the only way to finance a home. It became the standard product because it generates the most interest income for banks over the longest period of time, and because it was sold to the American public as a manageable monthly payment without much honest conversation about the total cost. You weren't asking what does this cost over its full life. You were asking can I afford this monthly. Those are two completely different questions, and the industry quietly hoped you'd only ever ask the second one.

You've now asked the first one. The rest of this book is the answer.

The Transparency Part

Before we go any further, I want to do something I believe every person in my industry should do and almost none of them actually do. I want to tell you exactly what I'm selling. And why.

This book exists because I'm a mortgage loan officer and I sell a product called a First Lien HELOC. Through my Keep The Cash Mortgage network and the loan officers I work with, this product is what the rest of this book is about. I'm telling you that right here, before I've earned a single dollar of your trust, because I spent seventeen years as a pastor before I ever became a loan officer, and I cannot write a book about financial transparency while hiding my own financial interest in what I'm describing.

So here it is: If you read this book and decide this strategy is right for your family, there's a real possibility you'll work with me or someone in my network. And we'll get paid. Fairly. Transparently. You'll know exactly what we're making.

But the math in this book is real whether you ever call me or not. The amortization numbers above are accurate. The alternatives I'm about to show you are real, available right now through licensed lenders across almost every state. You don't have to work with me to use this information.

No fog. No fine print. No number that should have been explained at closing but wasn't. That's what Keep The Cash Mortgage means.

Now you know the number on page five.

The next chapter is going to make you even madder. Because the answer to "does it have to be this way" isn't complicated, and it isn't hiding in some Wall Street back room. It's sitting in your paycheck right now. Floating in your checking account. Doing absolutely nothing while your mortgage balance accrues interest every single day.

Your own money is the answer. You just haven't been shown how to use it yet.

CHAPTER 2

Your Money Is Doing Nothing Right Now

Your paycheck hit this morning.

Maybe it was a direct deposit. Maybe it was two weeks of work showing up as a number on your phone at 6 a.m. while you were still in bed. You looked at it, felt that little pulse of relief the way you always do, and then got up and started your day.

And right now, at this very moment, that money is sitting in your checking account. Just… sitting there.

You're not going to pay most of your bills until the end of the week, or maybe the first of the month. Your mortgage payment doesn't draft until the 15th. Your utilities auto-pay on the 22nd. The grocery run hasn't happened yet. So for the next several days, maybe longer, that paycheck is parked in a checking account at a bank that is paying you somewhere between 0.01% and 0.5% interest on it, if they're paying you anything at all.

Meanwhile, somewhere else in that same bank's system, your mortgage balance is doing what it does every single day.

Accruing interest.

Not at 0.01%. Not at 0.5%. At whatever rate you signed for at closing. Six and a half percent. Seven percent. Seven and a quarter. Every day. On the full remaining balance. While your paycheck sits twenty feet away — or maybe in the very same building — earning almost nothing.

That gap right there — between what your idle money isn't earning and what your mortgage is costing you every day — is one of the quietest and most expensive things happening in your financial life. And almost nobody ever talks about it.

The Daily Float

I want to talk about something the banking industry never, ever brings up in polite company. They'll talk to you all day about rates and terms and their app that lets you deposit a check by taking a picture of it. But they will not sit you down and explain what happens to your money in the time between when it lands in your account and when you spend it. That would be rude. Expensive for them, but rude. In the banking world, there's a concept called the float. It's the money that exists in transit — deposited but not yet spent. And for the average American household, the float is substantial.

Think about your own account right now. After your paycheck lands and before you've paid everything out, how much is sitting there? If you're like most families, somewhere between $2,000 and $8,000 is parked in checking at any given point in the month. Some months more, some less. The exact number doesn't matter for right now. What matters is that it's there, it's real, and it is not working.

Your bank knows this. That's why they love checking accounts. Your money sits in their system, they lend it out to other people at real interest rates, and they pay you somewhere between nothing and embarrassing to let them use it. It's an entirely legal arrangement. It's also a pretty good deal for them and a lousy one for you.

But here's what really gets me. The money that's sitting idle in your checking account? It's not just earning nothing. It's costing you something. Because the whole time it's parked there doing nothing, you have a mortgage balance that is running up a tab against you. Every single day.

WHAT YOUR MORTGAGE COSTS YOU EVERY DAY	$400,000 @ 6.5%
Annual interest (year 1)	$25,868
Monthly interest charge (year 1)	$2,148
Daily interest charge (year 1)	$70.62
While your paycheck sits for 7 days	$494 gone
While your paycheck sits for 14 days	$988 gone
Checking account earning on $5,000 (0.01%)	$0.50 / year

Let that land for a second. Seventy dollars a day. Before coffee. Before you've looked at your phone. The bank has already added seventy bucks to your tab and you haven't done a single thing yet except exist in a house you thought you owned. I don't know about you, but knowing that number changed how I felt about sitting in my living room. And while that's happening, your paycheck is sitting in a checking account earning less than a dollar a year.

Not a dollar a day. A dollar a year.

I'm not telling you this to make you feel bad about your bank. I'm telling you this because that gap is the thing we're going to close.

And when you understand the gap, what comes next makes complete sense.

You Probably Earn More Than You Owe

Here's the thing about your mortgage that the bank is counting on you never to fully reckon with.

You borrowed $400,000 once. One time. And now you're paying it back over 30 years. But in those 30 years, most households will earn somewhere between $2 million and $5 million in gross income. The money that flows through your life over the next three decades absolutely dwarfs the mortgage balance that's sitting on your home.

The problem isn't the amount of money. The problem is the timing.

That money comes in little chunks. Biweekly paychecks. Monthly deposits. Commission checks that land and then wait. Every time a dollar comes in, it lands in a checking account that is completely disconnected from the mortgage balance it could be reducing. The income and the debt exist in separate systems. They never meet. The checking account earns nothing. The mortgage charges daily. And you make a payment once a month that the amortization schedule is specifically designed to keep tilted in the bank's favor for as long as possible.

What if they weren't separate?

What if every dollar that hit your account hit your mortgage balance at the same moment — reducing what you owe, reducing what the bank charges you tomorrow, and staying available to spend when you actually need it?

That's not a hypothetical. That's a product that exists right now.

But I'm getting ahead of myself. Before I show you the mechanism, I want to make sure the problem is real to you. Because if you take one thing from this chapter, it's this:

The Bank Gets Paid Every Day. You Only Get Credit Once a Month.

A traditional mortgage calculates your interest monthly, based on the balance at the start of the month. Your payment counts once — on whatever day it's due. No matter when you deposit money, no matter how much sits in your account, your mortgage balance doesn't move until that scheduled payment posts.

The bank's meter runs every day. Yours resets once a month. That's not an accident. That's the design.

Think about what that actually means for your paycheck situation. You get paid on the 1st and the 15th. Your mortgage payments on the 1st. So your paycheck lands — your mortgage takes its cut — and the remainder sits in checking for two weeks doing nothing until the cycle repeats. You're never late. You're never behind. You're doing everything right.

And still, every single day, the bank adds another $70 to your tab. Because that's how the math is built. Your money waits for permission to help you. Their interest doesn't wait for anything.

What the Idle Money Is Actually Costing You

I want to run a number that most people have never seen. Not the total interest over 30 years — we covered that in Chapter 1 and it's already burned into your brain. This is a different number. This is what the timing gap costs you. The gap between when your money arrives and when it actually reduces your debt.

The average American household has a checking account balance of roughly $5,500 at any given time, according to the Federal Reserve's Survey of Consumer Finances. Not savings, not investments — just the money sitting in checking, waiting to be spent.

Now here's what that $5,500 would do if it were applied to a 6.5% mortgage balance instead of sitting in a checking account earning 0.01%:

THE COST OF IDLE MONEY	$5,500 for 30 Days
Interest earned in checking at 0.01% APY	$0.05
Interest your mortgage saved if applied to balance	$29.79
Net difference (what the idle money cost you)	$29.74 / month
That same gap over 12 months	$356.88
That same gap over 10 years	$3,568.80
Compounded across the full mortgage term	$8,200+ lost

Eight thousand dollars. Lost. Not to a bad investment. Not to a scam. Not to a financial crisis. Lost to the timing gap between when your money arrived and when your mortgage would actually use it. And that's just the idle checking account balance. That doesn't count the paycheck that lands two weeks before you need to spend it, or the commission check that sits for three weeks, or the tax refund that floats for a month before you figure out what to do with it.

Add all of those up and you're not talking about $8,000. You're talking about real money. Money that has been financing the bank's operation instead of your freedom.

This Isn't About Discipline. It's About Design.

I need to say something before we get to the solution, because I've had this conversation at enough kitchen tables to know where people's minds go when they start to understand the problem.

They think: I need to be better with money. They think about budgeting apps and spending freezes and transferring money manually to make extra principal payments. They think the problem is their behavior.

It's not. Or rather — it's not only your behavior. The bigger problem is the design of the system you're working inside. A traditional mortgage is designed to disconnect your income from your debt. That's not an oversight. That's the architecture. The bank doesn't want your $5,500 in checking sitting next to your mortgage balance every day. If it did, it would have built a product that worked that way. It didn't. You got a mortgage and a checking account. Two separate things. Two separate systems. One earning almost nothing, one charging you daily.

People who make extra principal payments every month are doing something smart and genuinely helpful. I'm not knocking it. But they're also doing it manually, every month, with discipline that most people can't maintain forever. Life happens. The extra payment you were going to make in March got eaten by the car repair. The one in July got eaten by the vacation you needed. And you're back to making one payment a month, watching the amortization schedule do its slow, steady, bank-friendly work.

What if the system itself was built to deploy your money the moment it arrived?

What if there was no manual step? No discipline required? No extra payment to remember to make? What if your paycheck hit, your balance dropped automatically, and the bank started charging you less interest tomorrow — without you doing a single thing differently than you do right now?

That's what we're about to talk about. Your money has been doing nothing for years.

Not because you're bad with money. Not because you didn't care enough. Because nobody built you a system where it could do anything else. You had a checking account and you had a mortgage and they never touched each other. The income and the debt lived completely separate lives, and the only one that benefited from that arrangement was the bank.

The next chapter is where that changes. I'm going to show you exactly how a First Lien HELOC works — not in banker language, not in a brochure, but the way I explain it when I'm sitting at someone's kitchen table and they're looking at me like they want to make absolutely sure I'm not about to sell them something. I'm going to show you the mechanics, the math, the honest caveats, and why the single most important thing about this product isn't the rate.

It's the design.

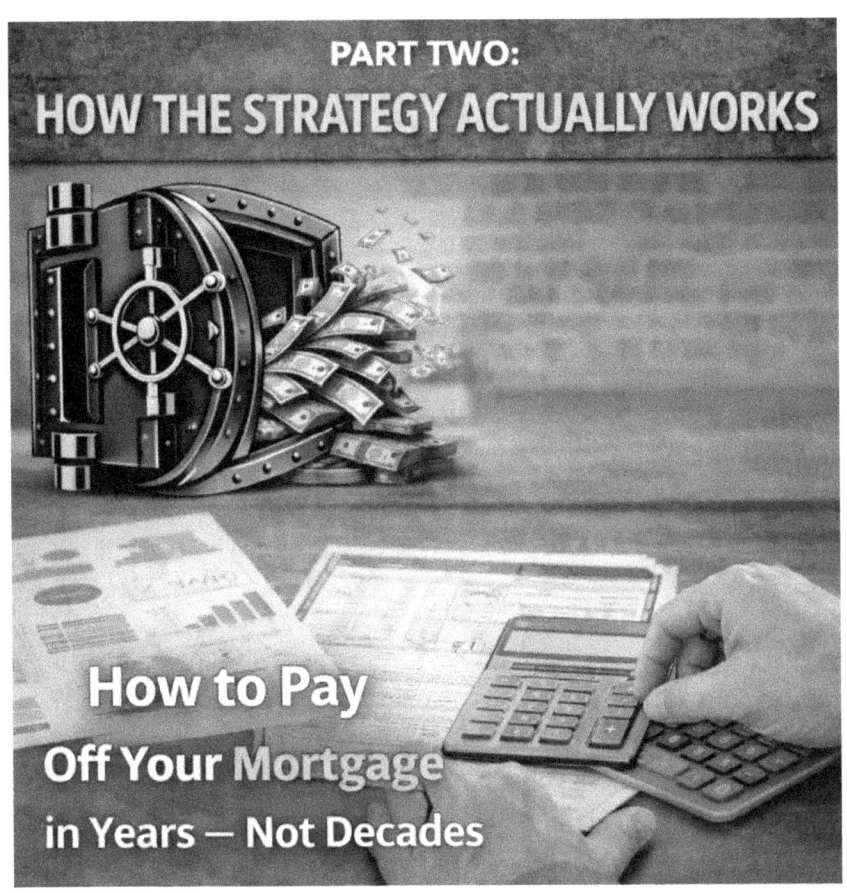

PART TWO:

HOW THE STRATEGY ACTUALLY WORKS

How to Pay Off Your Mortgage in Years — Not Decades

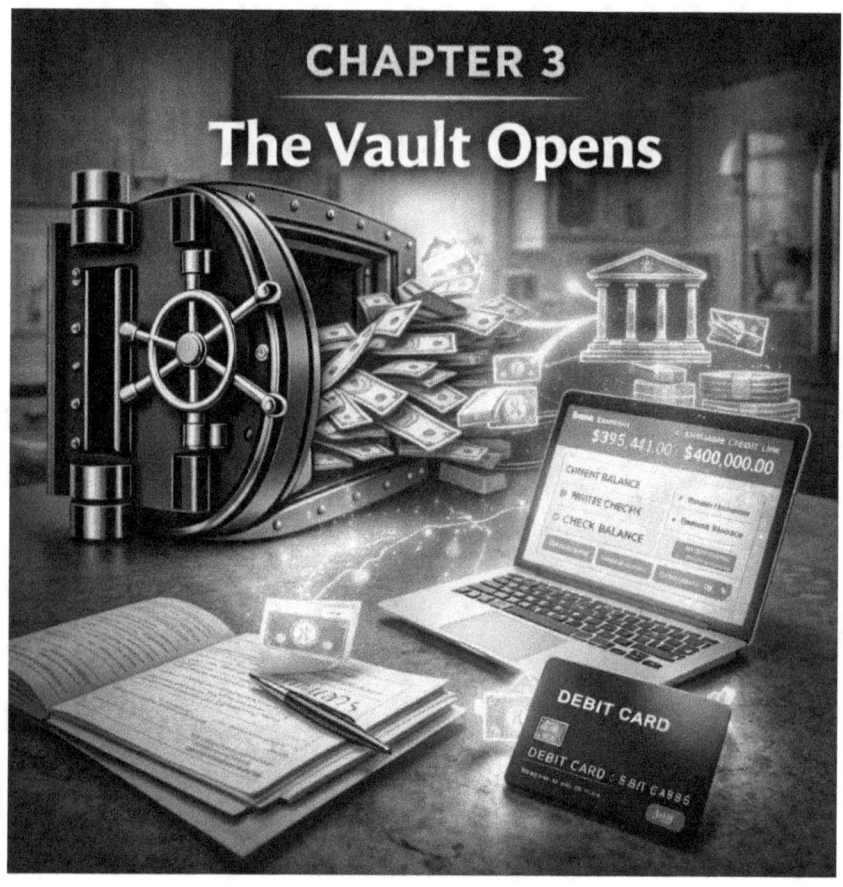

CHAPTER 3
The Vault Opens

I've sat across a lot of kitchen tables in this business.

Some of them are fancy — granite countertops, the whole thing. Some of them are the same kind my grandmother had, with the vinyl chairs that make that little squeak when you shift in your seat. Doesn't matter. The conversation's always the same. The homeowner across from me has a legal pad. Maybe they printed something off the internet. Maybe they've got my calculator results sitting in front of them with the savings number circled twice and a question mark next to it.

And they look at me and they say some version of the same thing every time.

"Okay. Explain it to me like I'm not a loan officer."

I've heard that exact sentence at more kitchen tables than I can count. And I always think: yes. Finally. That's the right question. Because "explain it like I'm a loan officer" gets you a brochure. "Explain it like I'm not" gets you the truth.

That's this chapter. Right here. You, me, kitchen table. No brochure language, no loan disclosure, no paragraph that starts with "pursuant to the terms of." Just the actual thing — how it works, why it works, and what it's going to do to that number you saw at the bottom of your amortization table.

Because here's what I've learned sitting at those tables: people don't need more information. They've got plenty of information. What they need is for someone to just slow down and tell them the truth in plain English.

So that's what we're going to do.

Start Here: Forget Everything the Word "HELOC" Made You Think Of

When most people hear "HELOC," they picture a second mortgage. And honestly, can you blame them? HELOC sounds like something a doctor would find on an X-ray. "Mr. Dendy, we've got a HELOC on your left side, but don't worry, we can treat it with a second mortgage and some paperwork." The name does not help. I didn't name it. If I had, I'd have called it something like the Freedom Account or the Get Out of Debt Faster Thing. But nobody asked me. So people hear the word and picture the old version — a thing you bolt on top of your existing loan... You keep your regular mortgage, you add a line of credit on top of it, and now you've got two payments and twice the paperwork.

That's a HELOC. But that is not what we're talking about.

A First Lien HELOC is different in one very specific and very important way.

It *replaces* your current mortgage entirely.

Not on top of it. Not alongside it. Instead of it. Your existing mortgage goes away. The First Lien HELOC becomes your mortgage — the primary, first-position lien on your home. Same house. Same ownership. Completely different financial architecture underneath it.

That distinction matters more than anything else in this chapter, so read it again if you need to. We're not adding debt. We're replacing debt. And replacing it with something built differently — designed to work with your income instead of against it.

What It Actually Is

Here's how I explain it when someone's looking at me with that "I want to believe you but I've been sold things before" look on their face.

A First Lien HELOC is a mortgage that also works like a checking account.

That's it. That's the whole thing. Your paycheck goes in. Your bills go out. The difference — every dollar that's sitting in there between when money arrives and when you spend it — is grinding down your principal balance every single day.

Not once a month. Not on a payment schedule. Every day.

Let me walk through the mechanics plain, because this is where people's eyes either light up or go a little glazed, and I need yours to light up.

When you close on a First Lien HELOC, your lender establishes a line of credit based on your home's appraised value minus what you owe. If your home is worth $500,000 and you have a $350,000 mortgage balance, that's roughly $150,000 in available equity. They'll advance the current balance, pay off your existing mortgage in full, and your new credit limit is set at that balance.

From there, you get a debit card. Check writing. Bill pay. Mobile banking. ACH transfers. Everything your regular checking account has…except this account is also your mortgage. You should have seen Bo's face when I told her that her checking account was her mortgage. I've explained a lot of complicated things at a lot of kitchen tables. That one took a minute. You point your direct deposit here instead of to a separate bank.

Your paycheck hits the account. Immediately, your outstanding balance drops. And here's the part that makes the whole thing click: because interest on a First Lien HELOC accrues daily on the actual outstanding balance — not on a fixed monthly schedule, not on what you owed at the start of the month, but on what you literally owe right now, this morning — a lower balance means lower interest charged tomorrow. Automatically. Without you doing anything.

You spend throughout the month. Groceries, utilities, car payment, whatever you do. Now, I've got twelve kids, so when I say "groceries" I mean we basically have a standing reservation at Costco. We're on a first-name basis with the people in the warehouse section. The point is, it doesn't matter if your grocery bill is $200 or $2,000. Everything goes through the same account. You spend, the balance goes up a little. Paycheck hits, it goes back down. Each purchase draws from the account, balance goes up a little, interest charge adjusts accordingly. Then your next paycheck hits and the balance drops again.

The surplus — the gap between what you earn and what you spend is sitting in that account working against your balance instead of sitting in a checking account earning a rounding error.

That's the mechanism. That's the whole machine.

The problem is that most people hear it and think about their budget. I'm showing you that the mortgage itself, the biggest line item in your financial life, has a version that actually does this automatically. Your money goes in. It works for you the second it arrives. No manual step. No willpower required.

The Design Difference, Side by Side

I want to show you the two designs next to each other, because once you see them laid out this way, you can't unsee it.

	Traditional 30-Year Mortgage	First Lien HELOC
How interest calculates	Monthly, on opening balance	Daily, on actual balance
When your payment counts	Once a month, on due date	Every day, in real time
Where your paycheck lives	Separate checking account	In the account reducing your balance
Idle money doing nothing	Yes — all of it, all month	No — it's working the moment it lands
Access to your equity	Locked — refinance or sell	Available — write a check
Extra payments required?	Manual, on top of regular payment	Built into the design — no extra step
Designed around	The bank's schedule	Your cash flow

The bank's schedule. That's the thing that gets me every time I look at that table. Your 30-year mortgage was not designed with your cash flow in mind. It was designed with a payment schedule that maximizes the amount of time your money is separated from your debt. That's not cynicism — that's just how amortization math works. The bank gets interest calculated monthly on the full opening balance. You get credit for your payment once a month. Everything in between, they keep.

A First Lien HELOC flips that architecture. It says: your income should start working the second it arrives. The idle gap between paycheck and payment shouldn't exist. Your money should be in the same place as your debt, reducing what you owe, every single day.

The One Number That Changes Everything

There's a number called your Average Daily Balance. And in a First Lien HELOC, it is the single most important thing happening in your financial life.

Here's the simple version: your interest charge for any given month is calculated by multiplying your average daily balance times your daily rate times the number of days in the month.

Average. Daily. Balance.

Not your balance on the first of the month. Not your balance when you make a payment. The average of what you owed each day, all the way through.

This is why the deposit timing matters so much. On a traditional mortgage, it doesn't matter whether your paycheck hits your bank on the 2nd or the 28th — your mortgage interest is calculated on the balance at the start of the billing cycle and it doesn't change until you make your scheduled payment. The bank doesn't care what's sitting in your checking account. They've already set the meter.

On a First Lien HELOC, the meter resets every single day. When your paycheck lands on the 2nd and drops your balance by $4,500, that $4,500 is reducing your average daily balance for the rest of the month. And a lower average daily balance means a lower interest charge. Which means more of every dollar you put in goes toward principal. Which means your balance drops faster. Which means next month's average daily balance starts lower. Which means...

You see how this builds on itself.

The traditional mortgage is designed to slow that momentum down. The First Lien HELOC is designed to let it run.

What About the Variable Rate — Let's Talk About That Right Now

I know it's in your head. It was in mine too, the first time I sat down with this product. And I'd rather just deal with it here than let it sit in the back of your mind making you nervous through the next two chapters.

Yes. A First Lien HELOC has a variable rate. It is tied to an index — currently SOFR, the Secured Overnight Financing Rate — that adjusts periodically as market conditions change. It is not a fixed rate mortgage. The rate you start with is not guaranteed to be the rate you finish with.

That's real, and I'm not going to spin it.

But here's what I need you to understand — and this is the thing people miss when they hear "variable rate" and immediately picture themselves underwater: the payoff speed of this strategy is not primarily driven by the rate.

It's driven by the gap between what you earn and what you spend.

Your surplus — the difference between your monthly net income and your monthly expenses — is your weapon. That surplus is what parks in the account, reduces your average daily balance, and accelerates your payoff. A rate adjustment makes the weapon a little lighter or a little heavier, but it doesn't take the weapon away.

Let me show you what I mean with real numbers. Take a $400,000 balance at a starting rate of 7%, with a household net income of $9,000 a month and expenses of $3,500. Monthly surplus of $5,500.

HELOC Rate Scenario	Payoff Timeline	Total Interest Paid	vs. 30-Year Fixed
7.00% (starting rate)	6 yrs 1 mo	$76,400	Saves $431,600
8.00% (+1 point)	6 yrs 8 mo	$87,200	Saves $420,800
9.00% (+2 points)	7 yrs 3 mo	$99,600	Saves $408,400
10.00% (+3 points)	7 yrs 11 mo	$114,100	Saves $393,900

Even if rates climbed three full points from today — which would be a significant and historically unusual rate environment — you're still paying off a $400,000 mortgage in under 8 years and saving nearly $400,000 in interest compared to the 30-year path.

The rate matters. I'm not saying it doesn't. But it's not the thing that breaks the strategy. What breaks the strategy is spending more than you make. What breaks the strategy is drawing the balance back up every time you see a zero. The math is remarkably durable against rate movement. It is not durable against behavior that works against it.

We'll talk more about that in Chapter 6. For right now, just sit with this: the variable rate is a real thing to understand and plan for. It is not a reason to hand the bank another 20 years of interest.

The Equity Access Nobody Talks About

There's a benefit to this structure that doesn't get nearly enough airtime, and I want to make sure you understand it because it changes how you think about the whole thing.

When you build equity in a traditional mortgage, that equity is locked. It's your money — technically — but you can't touch it without a cash-out refinance, a home equity loan, or selling the house. Want to access $40,000 for a roof? Better call a lender, start an application, wait for an appraisal, and pay closing costs. And if rates have moved, you might be refinancing your whole mortgage into a less favorable position just to get at your own equity.

With a First Lien HELOC, the equity you build stays liquid. If you've paid your balance down from $400,000 to $280,000, you have $120,000 available on that line of credit. You want $40,000 for the roof? Write a check. It's done. The balance goes back up to $320,000 and you start grinding it back down. No application. No appraisal. No closing costs. No locked-in rate change.

Bo and I have been doing this long enough to know that life doesn't stay in a straight line. Twelve kids have a way of rearranging your financial plans on a pretty regular schedule. The ability to access built equity without a second transaction isn't just a nice feature — it's a real safety valve. It's the difference between an emergency fund that earns nothing in a savings account and an emergency fund that's actually reducing your mortgage balance until the moment you need it.

What the Industry Doesn't Tell You About Why This Exists

Here's something worth understanding before we go any further.

Products like the First Lien HELOC aren't new. Programs built on this same architecture have existed for years. They've been wildly successful in Australia and the United Kingdom — where they're called offset mortgages — for decades. In those markets, this type of product is standard. Mainstream. What most homeowners use.

In the United States, they represent a tiny fraction of originations.

Not because they don't work. They work. The math is real and it's been proven. Not because they're not available. They're available through licensed lenders in most states right now. Because the mortgage industry in this country is built around a product — the 30-year fixed — that generates the maximum possible interest income over the maximum possible timeline.

A First Lien HELOC that pays off in 6 years generates 6 years of interest. A 30-year fixed generates 30 years. You do the math on what that means for the industry's revenue model, and you'll understand pretty quickly why nobody's been sending you a brochure about this.

That's not a conspiracy. That's just business. The bank is a business. Their product lineup reflects what makes them money, not what saves you money. And they're banking — no pun intended — on the fact that you'll keep doing what everyone around you does, which is sign a 30-year mortgage and make the payments and figure the interest is just the cost of having a house.

It doesn't have to be.

The Tagline That Earns Its Keep

I've been saying some version of this for years now, and I'm going to put it right here because it's as accurate a summary of this whole chapter as I can give you:

Your income is bigger than your mortgage debt. The First Lien HELOC just lets them meet.

— **Michael Dendy**

That's not marketing. That's arithmetic.

The average household earning $8,000 to $12,000 a month net doesn't have a small income problem. They have a design problem. The money comes in and it parks somewhere that doesn't talk to the debt. The checking account and the mortgage live separate lives. The income never meets the balance. And the bank collects interest on the full amount, every day, because the architecture keeps them apart.

Change the architecture, and the math changes with it. Not because you're earning more. Not because you're spending less. Just because the money you already have is finally in the same place as the debt it could be eliminating.

That's the vault opening. Right there.

The next chapter is where we run the numbers on a real person, not a hypothetical, not generic scenario, a person with real balances and real income and a real family. And I'm going to show you what the difference actually looks like on paper. Because understanding the mechanism is one thing.

Seeing your own number is something else entirely.

That's when it gets personal.

CHAPTER 4
The Numbers Don't Lie
(And Neither Do I)

First Lien HELOC
$58k Interest Paid
Payoff Age 47

Traditional Mortgage
$640k Interest Paid
Payoff Age 64

I'm not going to ask you to take my word for any of this.

That's not how I do business, and honestly, it's not how you should make a decision of this size anyway. I've got twelve kids — I've had to figure out the difference between a slick pitch and an honest deal more times than I can count. You shouldn't trust a number you can't trace. So this chapter is the trace.

I'm going to walk you through a client scenario and I'm going to show you the actual math. Not the headline number. The mechanism. Why it works, how it builds, and what it means for a real human life on the other side of it.

If you see yourself in this story, good. That's the point. And when you're done reading, I'm going to tell you exactly where to go punch in your own numbers. Because your number is the only one that's going to matter at two in the morning when you're sitting there deciding whether to make the call.

A Client Named Joel

Joel called me on a Friday. I remember because I was already juggling three other files and I almost let it go to voicemail. Glad I didn't.

He was 57, moving to Tennessee from out of state, and he'd already sold his place. Had a good chunk of cash in hand from the sale — enough to put 25% down on a $507,000 house, which meant his loan amount was going to be $380,000. He was the kind of guy who'd done the work, saved the money, done everything right. He just wanted to know his options before he signed anything.

So I laid them out. I showed him the traditional routes — 30-year fixed, 15-year fixed, the usual lineup. And then I showed him this.

	First Lien HELOC	Traditional Mortgage
Payoff timeline	6 years, 2 months	30 years
Total interest paid	$80,929	$508,069

Interest saved	$427,140	—
Age at payoff	63	87
Time saved	23 years, 10 months	—
Per day saved	$195	—

I walked him through the daily interest math. Showed him how his paycheck sitting in a checking account was costing him money every single day it wasn't applied to his balance. Showed him what his surplus, the $6,000 a month between what he earns and what he spends, would do inside a First Lien HELOC versus what it would do parked in a regular account next to a traditional mortgage.

He got quiet. Not confused quiet. The other kind.

Then he said, "Run that again."

So I did. Same numbers. Same result. And he sat with it for a second and then said he didn't want to hear about the other options anymore. He wanted that one.

I'll be honest...he still had questions. Variable rate. Closing costs. What happens if something goes sideways. All the right questions, and we answered every one of them. But the reason he kept coming back to this product wasn't that I'm a great salesman. It was that the math is hard to argue with once you actually see it.

Here's what Joel's situation looked like on paper.

Joel — Age 57

Mortgage balance: **$380,000**

Rate: **6.75%**

Years remaining: **26 years**

Net monthly income: **$9,800**

Monthly expenses: **$3,800**

Monthly surplus: **$6,000**

Why the Surplus Is the Whole Story

I want to go back to something before we move on, because I think it's the thing that gets missed when people look at these numbers and focus on the savings number.

The savings number is real. But it's not the driver. The driver is the surplus.

This specific 1ˢᵗ Lien HELOC runs on an engine. Income comes in. Expenses go out. The difference parks in the HELOC account and grinds the balance down every single day. The bigger the surplus, the faster the grind. The more consistent the surplus, the more reliable the payoff timeline.

This is why I said in Chapter 2 that the problem isn't income. Most people that qualify for a mortgage already earn more than they owe, they just earn it over time in small chunks that park somewhere useless between arrival and when they get spent. A First Lien HELOC doesn't require you to earn more. It doesn't require you to spend less. It just requires you to park your money in the right account.

The behavior change is small. The result is enormous. That's the compounding idea of doing just the right small thing consistently.

Your surplus is your rate of payoff. *The HELOC is just the vehicle.*

That's why I always ask a borrower two questions before I run their numbers if they are considering this as an option. Not "what's your credit score" that comes later. First two questions are: what's your take-home every month, and what do you actually spend? The gap between those two numbers is what determines everything else. That gap is the engine. I'm just handing them the car.

Now Run Your Own

I've shown you Joel's story. His story is not you. Your balance is different. Your rate is different. Your income is different. The number that's going to matter to you, the one you'll circle on the page or screenshot on your phone is your number.

So go get it.

KeepTheCash.com/heloc-calculator. Put in your balance, your rate, your years remaining, your income, your expenses. Let it run. The calculator will show you your payoff timeline on the HELOC path, your total interest on both paths, and the interest you'd save.

Don't take my numbers for it. Punch in yours. I'll wait.

When you see your own number, not someone else's, the rest of this book is going to land differently. Because right now you're reading about Joel. But in about five minutes, you're going to be reading about yourself.

And that's when the questions start. Good questions. The kind I want you asking. The kind where you look at the calculator results and you go: okay, but what about the variable rate, and what does it cost to set this up, and what happens if I lose my job.

Those are exactly the five questions the next chapter is going to answer. Straight. No spin. The way I'd answer them if you were sitting across from me right now with your calculator printout and your legal pad, ready to get into it.

Let's get into it.

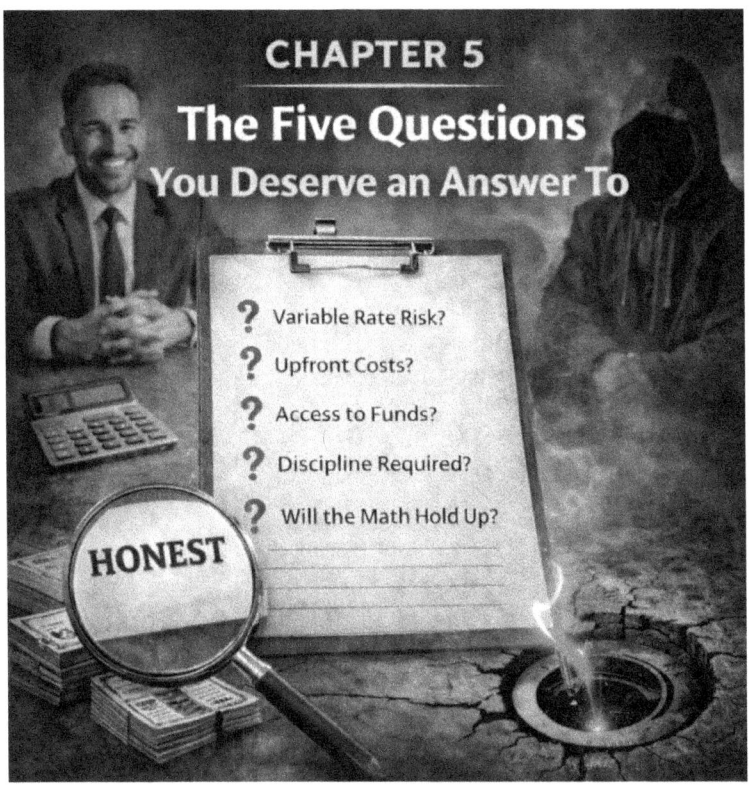

I've been doing this long enough to know when someone has questions they're not asking yet.

They're sitting there with the calculator printout. The numbers are good, they can see that. The savings number is circled. The payoff timeline has an asterisk next to it and a question mark. And there's something behind their eyes that says: this is too good. What am I missing?

Good. That's the right instinct. That's the instinct that protects you in every financial decision you'll ever make. Don't let a number dazzle you into skipping the hard questions.

So let's do the hard questions. Right here, right now, before we go any further. I've sat at enough kitchen tables to know exactly which five questions are coming. And I'd rather answer them honestly in this chapter than have you find out the answers later from someone with less of a reason to be straight with you.

There are no trick answers in here. There are a couple of honest answers that won't sound great at first. That's fine. The goal isn't to make this strategy sound perfect. The goal is to make sure you understand it completely before you decide if it's right for you.

That's what this chapter is. Not a sales close. Not a list of objections I'm going to knock down with a smile. Just the honest information you need to decide for yourself.

Variable rates scare me

Maybe you're thinking, "Is the variable rate going to kill me?" The transparent and honest answer... Maybe. If you don't understand how this strategy actually works.

I'm not going to soften that. A First Lien HELOC carries a variable rate tied to SOFR — the Secured Overnight Financing Rate — and it adjusts periodically as market conditions move. It is not a 30-year fixed. The rate you start with is not the rate you're guaranteed to finish with. If rates go up, your HELOC gets more expensive. That's real, and anybody who tells you different is either confused or selling something.

Here's the thing people miss when they hear "variable rate" and their stomach drops:

The payoff speed of this strategy is not primarily driven by the rate. **It's driven by the gap between what you earn and what you spend.**

We covered this in Chapter 3 and showed it in the stress test table. But since this is the question that keeps more people up at night than any other, let me run it one more time, plainly. Go look back at the table in Chapter 3.

A three-point rate jump — which would be a historically significant and unusual rate environment — adds less than two years to the payoff timeline and still results in nearly $393,900 in savings compared to finishing a 30-year mortgage. The rate is a headwind, not a wall.

But here's where I have to be honest with you about something else, because I said I would be.

If a rate increase would genuinely put you underwater on this strategy — if your surplus is thin enough that a couple of rate points would erase it entirely — then you should not do this strategy right now. Not everyone is a fit. A borrower with a $200 monthly surplus has almost no cushion against rate movement. A borrower with a $4,000 monthly surplus has a lot. Your loan officer should run your stress test before you sign anything. At Keep The Cash, we do that math first. Every time. If the numbers don't hold up under rate pressure, we tell you.

The variable rate is a real consideration. It is not a reason to spend 24 more years paying a bank $70 a day. But it is a reason to go in with your eyes open, and to make sure your surplus is real before you commit.

How much does it cost?

Some clients just want to know how much it is going to cost to set this type of loan up. If that's you, I can tell you that it's not hundreds of thousands of dollars and it's not free.

My grandfather, we called him "Pappy" used to say "nothing in life is free except the sunrise, and some people would charge you for that if they could figure out how." He was talking about something else entirely. I think it was a neighbor of his. But he was also accidentally describing the mortgage industry. This is not free. I want to say that loudly and upfront, because the interest savings number is so large that people sometimes assume the setup cost must be negligible. It's not nothing.

Closing costs on a First Lien HELOC are comparable to a standard refinance. You're looking at roughly 2 to 3 percent of the loan amount in most cases, depending on the lender, your state, the property, and the specific program.

So there's a break-even point. The interest savings you're generating from day one of the strategy need to outpace those upfront closing costs before you're in the black. In most scenarios I run, that break-even point lands somewhere between 8 and 18 months. By month 15, the interest you're not paying has typically covered what you spent to get in.

After that? Every month is money that used to go to the bank staying in your pocket instead.

But here's the rule I want you to hold onto:

Any loan officer who won't show you the break-even calculation before you sign is not the right loan officer.

That number should be on the table before the closing disclosure is. If someone is trying to get you to sign on the savings number alone without showing you what it costs to get there and exactly when you recoup it, walk away. That's not transparency. That's a pitch.

We show the break-even first. Before the savings. Before the payoff timeline. Before we talk about anything else. Because if the break-even doesn't work for your situation — if you're planning to sell in 14 months, if the closing costs are disproportionate to your balance, if something doesn't add up — then the conversation stops there. You deserve to know that before you spend a dime.

What if my income changes?

Clients ask me all the time, "What if my income drops?" This is the one that's really a life question dressed up as a financial question.

It's not really about the HELOC. It's about what happens when the plan meets reality — job loss, a medical event, a business that has a bad year, a spouse who stops working. And the honest answer is that if your income drops significantly and your expenses don't drop with it, the strategy slows down. Sometimes substantially.

That's just math. Your surplus is the engine. Shrink the surplus and you slow the engine. If the surplus goes to zero, the payoff acceleration stops entirely. You're still making a payment — you're just making the minimum interest payment on a variable rate line of credit instead of accelerating toward zero.

That's not catastrophe. But it's important to understand clearly.

Here's what the HELOC structure does provide that a traditional mortgage doesn't, and this matters for exactly this scenario:

There is no prepayment penalty. If your income drops and you need to slow down, you slow down. Nobody is charging you for the aggressive payments you made in the good months.

The equity you've built is accessible. If you've paid your balance from $400,000 down to $280,000 and a medical emergency hits, that $120,000 in available credit is right there. Write a check. No application, no appraisal, no new closing costs. You draw from your own equity and start rebuilding.

The flexibility runs both ways. When your income recovers, you go back to depositing your full paycheck and the acceleration picks back up. You haven't lost the strategy — you've paused it.

What I tell borrowers with variable or commission-based income is this: your loan officer needs to understand how your income actually moves before recommending this product. The strategy is built around a consistent surplus. If your income swings by $3,000 a month depending on whether it was a good quarter, that swing is part of the calculation. A good loan officer builds that into the analysis. A bad one shows you the best-case scenario and doesn't mention the rest.

I've got twelve kids. I understand variable cash flow in a way that's not theoretical. There are months where I've looked at the bank account and the number was concerning enough that I started counting ketchup packets in the junk drawer like they were assets. Variable cash flow is not an abstract concept in my house. It's a lifestyle. And here's what I've learned from it: the tool has to be flexible enough to handle real life, not just the version of life you described in the loan application. The months with unexpected expenses, the months where something big breaks, the years where the business is slow — life doesn't give you a straight line. The question isn't whether disruption will happen. It's whether the tool you're using is flexible enough to handle it when it does.

For most people with reasonably stable income and a real surplus, the answer is yes. For people with genuinely volatile income, this conversation needs to go deeper before you sign anything.

What about my equity?

Maybe you're worried you won't be able to access your equity. You can access your equity. And honestly, better than you can with a traditional mortgage. This is one of the structural advantages that doesn't get nearly enough airtime, maybe because it sounds too good and people assume there's a catch.

There's no catch.

With a traditional mortgage, the equity you build is yours in theory. In practice, it's locked inside the house. You cannot touch it without either selling the home, doing a cash-out refinance — which means new closing costs and likely a new rate — or opening a separate home equity loan or HELOC product on top of your existing mortgage. Every one of those options costs you time, money, or both.

With a First Lien HELOC, the equity you build stays liquid. If your balance is at $280,000 and your credit limit is $380,000, you have $100,000 sitting there available right now. Today. No application. No appraisal. No closing costs. You write a check or swipe a debit card and the money moves.

Bo and I bought our house in Georgia, moved to Michigan and landed in Tennessee. We've had years, between twelve kids and a mortgage business and a calling that doesn't always pay on schedule, where the ability to access equity without a new transaction was the difference between a manageable problem and a crisis. The flexibility isn't a gimmick. It's a real structural feature that changes how you think about your home equity.

Think about what that means in practice. You've been paying aggressively on the HELOC for three years. Your balance is down from $400,000 to $200,000. Your air conditioning unit dies, and the estimate to replace the whole system is $18,000. On a traditional mortgage, that $200,000 in equity is locked. You're calling a financing company, opening a personal loan, or putting it on a credit card at 21%. On a HELOC, you write an $18,000 check from your own equity at the HELOC rate. It's the same rate you're already paying on the mortgage and you keep grinding the balance down. No new debt. No new credit application. No 21% interest.

The line of credit stays open for the full 30-year term of the product. The equity you're building aggressively with this strategy doesn't disappear into a box you can't get into. It's right there, working for you until you need it.

Now — and I want to be direct about this — the accessible equity is also the place where the strategy can go sideways if you're not disciplined about it. We'll talk about that in Chapter 6. Access to equity is a safety valve, not a spending account. There's a version of this where someone pays the balance down aggressively for a year and then draws it back up to buy something they didn't need. That behavior destroys the math. Keep the draws for real needs and genuine emergencies, and the flexible equity stays a tool. Start treating it like a line of credit at a store and it becomes a problem.

More on that in the next chapter. Short answer to the question: yes, your equity stays accessible, and that's a feature, not a warning.

Why doesn't everyone do this?

Here is the biggest question that I get asked all the time when explaining this loan: Why doesn't everyone do this?

Because the industry has absolutely no financial incentive to tell you about it.

I know how that sounds. I know it sounds like the kind of thing someone says to make themselves sound like a whistleblower. I'm a mortgage loan officer. I'm not above the industry — I'm in it. But I also spent seventeen years as a pastor before I ever closed a mortgage loan, and I cannot explain this situation to you without just telling you the truth of it.

A 30-year fixed mortgage at $400,000 at 6.5% generates roughly $508,000 in interest over its full life. That's the bank's revenue from your loan. A First Lien HELOC on that same $400,000, paid off in six years, generates somewhere between $76,000 and $114,000 in interest depending on rate movement. That's the bank's revenue from your loan on this path.

The difference in revenue to the lender is somewhere around $400,000 per loan.

Think about that at scale. A lender doing 1,000 loans a year. That's four hundred million dollars in interest revenue the industry gives up if consumers understand this option and choose it. Banks are not in the business of losing four hundred million dollars per thousand loans. They're in the business of protecting their revenue model — legally, legitimately, and with complete indifference to whether it's in your best interest.

This isn't new information. Products built on this architecture have existed in the United States for years. They're available right now, through licensed lenders, in most states. They have been for a long time.

They just never got the marketing budget that the 30-year fixed gets. Because the 30-year fixed is what generates the most interest. And marketing budgets follow revenue.

Offshore, this is different. In Australia and the United Kingdom, the offset mortgage, which works on this same basic principle of keeping your income in the same place as your debt, is the dominant mortgage product. Most homeowners there use some version of this. It's considered standard. It's not exotic or niche. It's just how mortgages work there.

Here, the 30-year fixed became the standard because it was sold to the American public as the safe, responsible, manageable product. Monthly payment you can afford. Lock in your rate. Done. Nobody pointed out that "done" was going to take 30 years and cost you a second mortgage's worth of interest in the process.

I'm not the first person to figure this out. I'm probably not even the hundredth. But I do think I might be one of the louder people saying it plainly, in a book, with real numbers, to people who deserve to make this decision with full information.

That's why I built Keep The Cash. Not because I needed a new business model. Because I kept sitting at kitchen tables with people who were genuinely smart, genuinely hardworking, and genuinely unaware that they were handing hundreds of thousands of dollars to a bank that was counting on their not knowing any better. And at some point that stops being okay to just observe quietly.

So the answer to why doesn't everyone do this is simply: they don't know it exists. And the people who benefit most from them not knowing have the largest marketing budgets in the country.

Now you know.

Five questions. Five straight answers. No spin, no hedge, no fine print snuck in somewhere I hoped you wouldn't look.

The variable rate is real. The closing costs are real. The income risk is real. The equity access is real and it's actually better than what you have now. And the reason the industry doesn't hand you this information at closing is the same reason car dealerships don't show you the invoice price first — there's money in the gap between what you know and what they know.

The gap closes right here.

The next chapter is where I have to tell you something I genuinely mean: this strategy is not for everyone. I know that's an odd thing to say when I'm the person selling it. But a book that tells every reader they're the perfect candidate for any financial product is a book that's trying to sell something, not help someone. So Chapter 6 is where we talk about who this actually works for, who it doesn't, and how to know the difference before you pick up the phone.

That conversation is short. It's honest. And it might be the most useful thing in the book.

PART THREE:
GET TRANSPARENT ANSWERS
BEFORE YOU MOVE FORWARD

QUESTIONS TO ASK
☑ Variable Rate Risk?
☑ Upfront Costs?
☑ Access to Funds?
☑ Discipline Required?
☑ Will the Math Hold Up?

The Honest Answers You Need to a Different Mortgage Option and Its Real Risks

I want to tell you something before we go any further, and I want you to hear it in the spirit it's meant.

This strategy is not for everyone.

I know that's a strange sentence coming from the guy who wrote the book. But here's the thing: if I sat across from every single person who reads this and told them all the same thing — yes, this works for you, do it, call me — I'd be lying to some of them. And there are already enough people in the mortgage industry willing to do that. I've spent most of this book explaining how the industry profits from information that stays hidden. I'm not about to turn around and hide my own.

So this chapter is different from the others. This isn't me explaining why the strategy works. This is me telling you, as plainly as I can, exactly who it works for, exactly who it doesn't, and the specific things to look at in your own situation before you pick up the phone and start a conversation with a loan officer — mine or anyone else's.

A book that tries to be for everyone is a book trying to sell something. This book is trying to help someone. Those are different missions, and they lead to different chapters.

So let's be honest about the fit.

You can't make a good decision about a mortgage product until you're honest about your own financial situation. Not the version that sounds good in a loan application. The real one.

This Works Well When...

Let's start with the profile that makes this strategy perform. These aren't requirements in the legal sense — they're the conditions that make the math run well. Keep in mind, just because it says it is harder, doesn't mean it's impossible.

✓ The Strategy Works Well	✗ The Strategy Is Harder When
You have at least 15% equity in your home	You have less than 15% equity (LTV above 85%)
Your FICO score is 700 or above	Your FICO is below 700
You have stable, predictable monthly income	Your income varies significantly month to month

Your monthly expenses are less than your income — with real surplus	Your surplus is thin — under $500/month after all expenses
You plan to stay in the home at least 2–3 years	You're planning to sell in the next 12–18 months
You have the discipline to not spend down the available credit	You tend to treat available credit as available spending money
You understand variable rates and can handle rate movement	A rate increase of 2–3 points would erase your surplus
You're willing to treat the account like a mortgage, not a wallet	You're in Texas (specific state rules apply — call us first)

That table is the honest version of the pre-qualification conversation. Before the credit pull, before the application, before the rate quote — this is the real first question. Does your situation fit the conditions that make this strategy work?

Let me walk through the ones that matter most, because a few of them deserve more than a row in a table.

The Equity Threshold

Fifteen percent equity is not a preference — it's the qualification floor for a First Lien HELOC in most programs. That means your outstanding loan balance cannot exceed 85% of your home's current appraised value. If you bought recently with a small down payment, or if your market has pulled back since you purchased, you may not be there yet.

The fix for this isn't complicated. Wait. Keep making your mortgage payments. If your market is appreciating, you may hit the threshold faster than you think. If you've got some cash you could apply to principal, that could bridge the gap. The strategy doesn't go anywhere. When your equity position gets there, the numbers get run and the decision gets made.

Don't try to force a product into a situation where the math doesn't fit. Loan officers who let you do that aren't looking out for you. We'll tell you when it doesn't work and check back in when it might.

The Surplus Reality

This is the one I want to spend real time on, because it's where the most people fool themselves and not because they're trying to. It's because most of us don't actually know what we spend until we've tracked it for a couple of months.

I'll be honest with you about what happens at most of these initial conversations. I ask what they spend every month. They give me a number. It sounds reasonable. Then we go through it. We go through the Netflix, the Hulu, the gym they stopped going to in February, the subscriptions they forgot about, the coffee, the eating out, the thing that "comes up every month that always seems to come up". Then, the number grows. Not because they were lying. Because most of us have never actually added it all up. We know our mortgage payment. We know our car payment. The rest of life is a general feeling, not a number.

Here's the engine of this whole strategy: what you earn minus what you spend. That's it. That's the surplus number, and everything else runs on it. If that number is real and consistent, the math runs. If that number is optimistic, the math runs slower than projected. If that number is fictional, the strategy stalls and you've paid closing costs to end up in about the same place you started.

So here's what I ask every borrower to do before we run numbers together: spend two weeks tracking actual spending. Every dollar out. Add it up at the end. That's your expense number. Subtract it from your monthly net income. That's your real surplus.

The Behavior Question — And I Mean It

This is the one that's hardest to put in a table, because it's not about your credit score or your equity position or your income. It's about who you are when you see a number with a lot of zeros behind it.

A First Lien HELOC, once you've been paying aggressively for a year or two, will show you a growing available credit balance. Let's say you started at $380,000 and you've worked it down to $290,000. That means you have $90,000 available on the line of credit. Nine-zero thousand dollars, right there, accessible with a check or a debit card.

For some people, that number is invisible. They know it's there, they're glad it's there for emergencies, and they keep depositing paychecks and grinding the balance down without a second thought. That's the person this strategy was designed for.

For other people, $90,000 in available credit is $90,000 to spend. A kitchen they've been wanting. A boat. A boat. Lord have mercy, the number of financial strategies I have personally watched get sunk by a boat. Not even a big boat. Sometimes it's a jet ski. I have a theory that the boat industry is the single largest beneficiary of home equity products in America. I can't prove it. But I believe it in my heart. A trip to Europe that turned into a trip plus new luggage plus new gear plus two weeks off work without the income. Not because they're bad people. Because they grew up treating credit like cash and old habits don't disappear just because a book explained them.

If you are the second person — and only you know which one you are — this strategy will not work the way the math says it should. It's not that the math is wrong. It's that the behavior overrides the math. You'll pay the balance down, you'll draw it back up, and instead of an accelerating payoff you'll have an expensive revolving line of credit that you're very attached to.

I'm not judging that. I've got twelve kids. I've been the person in both columns at different points in my life. But I'm not going to sit across from you and tell you this product works the same for everyone when it demonstrably doesn't. The math requires the behavior. The behavior requires the honesty to know which category you're in.

Talk to your spouse about it. Talk to the person in your house who knows exactly how the credit cards get used. That conversation is worth having before the loan application conversation.

A Note on Any State With HELOC Restrictions

Texas has specific constitutional restrictions on home equity lending that affect how First Lien HELOC products work in that state. The rules aren't prohibitive — Texans can still access these products — but the requirements are different enough that I won't try to summarize them in a paragraph here and potentially give you incomplete information.

If you're in Texas, the conversation starts with the state-specific rules before it starts with the math. Call us. We'll walk through it correctly.

A handful of other states have their own nuances around HELOC products — restrictions on line of credit terms, requirements around draw periods, lender-specific limitations. Your loan officer should know these cold for your state. If they don't, that's important information about whether you're talking to the right loan officer.

The Timing Question — Don't Skip the Break-Even

We talked about the break-even in Chapter 5. I want to bring it back here because it intersects directly with the fit question.

If you're planning to sell your home in the next 12 to 18 months, the closing costs may not have time to recoup before the sale. The strategy depends on a break-even window. Most people hit that break-even somewhere between month 12 and month 18 depending on their balance, rate, and surplus. If you're out the door before then, you've spent money on closing costs and captured only a portion of the interest savings.

That's not a disaster — in most cases you'd still come out ahead of where you'd be on the traditional path, because the daily interest math starts working for you from day one. But the full benefit of the strategy requires time. If time is short, run the break-even analysis before you commit. Your loan officer should be running it with you regardless, but you should be asking for it specifically if your timeline is uncertain.

If you're staying put for three or more years with a real surplus and solid equity — the break-even isn't even really a question. The math overwhelms it quickly. But confirm it anyway. That's not paranoia. That's just due diligence.

So Where Does That Leave You?

Go back through this chapter and be honest with yourself about where you land. Not where you wish you were. Where you actually are.

Good equity position? Real surplus you've actually verified? Stable income? At least two or three years in the home? The discipline to treat available credit like a mortgage and not a debit card? If yes to most of those — run your numbers. The math is going to be worth the conversation.

Not there yet? Equity's thin, surplus is tight, income's variable, or the behavior question gave you a little pause? Sit with that honestly. This strategy doesn't expire. The numbers will still be here when your situation evolves. And knowing you're not quite ready is infinitely more valuable than signing a loan that doesn't fit because a book made it sound good.

That's the whole purpose of this chapter. Not to talk you out of it. To make sure that when you do it, you do it right — with full information, a real surplus, and eyes open on every part of the math.

The last chapter is the one I've been building toward since Chapter 1. It's not more numbers. It's not more mechanics. It's about what happens on the other side. What it actually feels like to sit in a house you own, completely, outright, no bank in the equation, before you ever thought that was possible.

That chapter is for Joel. And if your situation fits what we talked about in this chapter, it's for you too.

I want you to think about a Tuesday morning.

Ordinary Tuesday. Nothing special about it. You wake up, make the coffee, do the thing you do in those first fifteen minutes before the day starts pressing on you. Maybe you check your phone. Maybe you sit for a minute before the kids are up or the dog needs out or the schedule pulls you back into motion.

Now I want you to think about that same Tuesday morning, same house, same coffee, same fifteen minutes, except there is no mortgage payment this month. There wasn't one last month either.

Or the month before. The deed to the house is in a folder in your filing cabinet with your name on it and nobody else's. The bank is not in the equation.

How does that feel different?

Most people, when I ask them that question at a kitchen table, get quiet for a second. Not because it's a hard question. Because they've never actually let themselves sit in that version of Tuesday morning long enough to feel it. They've thought about paying off the mortgage the way you think about retirement, something that happens later, after years of doing the right thing, when you're old enough that the goal posts have already moved twice. Not something that happens at 47 or 54 or 40.

This chapter is about that Tuesday morning. What it actually means. Not the financial spreadsheet version, we've done that. The real version. The one that's about your life, not your amortization schedule.

The regret isn't usually about the risks you took. It's about the years you handed over to something that didn't have to take them. The twenty years of mortgage payments that felt mandatory when they weren't. The choices you didn't know you had. That's the thing that keeps people up at night when it's too late to do something about it, not that they tried and failed, but that they never knew to try.

You're reading this before it's too late. That matters.

Joel at 61

Let's go back to Joel from Chapter 4. Sixty-one years old now. Sixty-one. You know what sixty-one used to mean? Old. I have had family members that were done by sixty-one. Not done as in retired... done as in done. But sixty-one today is a man still in the middle of things. Still working. Still paying. Still planning. Still got at least one kid doing something that requires a phone call and a wire transfer, if my house is any indication. He would have twenty-six years left on a 30-year mortgage. When he was 57, he had two paths in front of him.

Joel	Traditional Path	Keep The Cash Path
Age at mortgage payoff	87 years old	64 years old
Years of payments remaining	26 years	6 years, 2 months
Total interest paid	$508,069	$80,929
Monthly surplus recaptured	At age 87	At age 64
Years to enjoy it	Retirement, if lucky	23+ years
Interest saved	—	$427,140

The savings number is $427,140. That's the headline. But let me tell you what $427,140 is not. It is not the most important thing in that table.

The most important thing in that table is the age at payoff.

Joel and his wife will be 64 when the mortgage is gone. They're still working and nearing retirement. They're not coasting into retirement, they're right in the middle of everything. And somewhere around month 74, the check they used to write every month to the bank stops leaving. Two thousand five hundred dollars a month, give or take. Just... doesn't go anywhere anymore.

That's $2,500 a month they get to decide what to do with. Not the bank. Not an amortization schedule. Them.

Some of it might go to a college fund or a wedding or a trip they have always wanted to take. Not a coincidence that's the life math that changes when the financial math changes. Some of it might go to retirement accounts that have been underfunded because the mortgage kept eating the surplus. Some of it might go to nothing, which is to say it just quietly makes every month easier. The family vacation doesn't require two months of planning around the budget. The car that needs replacing doesn't create a crisis. The margin that was always a little thin grows a little wide.

And they do this for twenty-three years before they'd have been done on the traditional path.

Twenty-three years of a mortgage payment they're keeping instead of sending. Do that math any way you want, invested, saved, spent on a life they were putting off and $427,140 in interest savings starts to look like the understatement of the chapter.

What I Know From My Own Kitchen Table

I'm going to get personal for a minute, because I think I owe you that after everything in this book.

Bo and I got married when I was 22 and she was 19. We were high school sweethearts out of Marietta, Georgia, the kind of Southern kids who grew up thinking that a house with a mortgage was just what responsible adults did. You buy a house, you get a mortgage, you pay it for thirty years. That's the plan. That was everybody's plan in Marietta. You didn't question it any more than you questioned sweet tea. It just came with the territory. You want a house? Here's your mortgage. You want something to drink? Here's your tea. Neither one of them comes with an explanation of the ingredients. That was the plan. Everybody's plan, far as we could tell.

We have twelve kids. Not a typo. Twelve. The house in Georgia, the house in Michigan and now the house in Tennessee has seen a lot of life. A lot of joy, a lot of chaos, a lot of months where the math was tight and we were grateful for every dollar we could account for. I was a pastor for seventeen years before I ever became a mortgage loan officer, and I can tell you that the conversations I had at kitchen tables as a pastor about money and fear and the weight of debt were not that different from the conversations I have now.

People carry their mortgages the way they carry a lot of hard things. Quietly. Like it's just the cost of having a life. They don't complain about it. They budget around it. They make it work. And somewhere in the back of their mind, if they're honest, they know the number is bigger than they're comfortable saying out loud.

I built Keep The Cash because I got tired of watching people do that. I got tired of sitting across from families who were doing everything right... working hard, spending carefully, saving what they could — and seeing them hand five hundred thousand dollars to a bank over thirty years because nobody ever sat them down and showed them the door.

The door was always there.

The math doesn't lie. The product exists. The strategy works when the conditions are right. I've watched it work. I've run the numbers for people at every age and income level and life situation in this book, and the pattern is the same: when the surplus is real and the behavior matches the math, the payoff timeline compresses in ways that feel almost too good to be true until you see the monthly statements.

But what I know from being a husband and a father and a pastor before I was a loan officer is that this isn't really about the money. Not at the bottom of it. The money is just the thing we're using to talk about the time.

The time with your kids while they're still at home. The years you don't have to choose between the job that pays the bills and the work you actually want to do. The retirement that isn't a financial scramble. The Tuesday morning where the coffee is still hot. I'm not writing this from the other side of a paid-off house. I'm writing it because I understand the math and I've watched it work for people and Bo and I are working our strategy ourselves right now.

That's what this is about. That's always what it's been about.

The Last Thing I'll Say

When I started writing Unlocked, I said the mortgage industry never told you how much you were really paying. In this book, I've tried to show you the way out.

Not a trick. Not a loophole. Just a different architecture for the same debt, one that's built around your cash flow instead of the bank's calendar. One that lets your income and your mortgage balance actually meet, every day, instead of living in separate systems that the bank designed to keep apart.

You've got the numbers now. You've got the mechanism. You've got five honest answers to the five hard questions. You've got a clear picture of who this fits and who it doesn't. And you've got a calculator at KeepTheCash.com/heloc-calculator that will show you your own number in about four minutes.

The only thing left is the decision.

Bo and I made ours. Joel made his before Social Security had a chance to show up and find him still making a payment.

What you do with all of this is yours. That's the point. That's always been the point.

The mortgage industry counted on you not knowing you had options.

Now you know.

Go keep your cash.

Appendix:

AM I READY? The One-Page Honest Self-Check

Before you call anybody, sit with these eight questions. Be honest. Not loan-application honest. Kitchen-table honest.

1. Do I have at least 15% equity in my home? That means your mortgage balance is no more than 85% of what the home is worth today. If you're not sure, a rough estimate works for now. You'll need a real appraisal later, but this tells you whether it's worth the conversation.

☐ Yes, I'm there.

☐ Not yet but I'm close.

☐ No, I need more time.

2. Is my FICO score 700 or above? Pull it before you call anyone. Know your number.

☐ Yes

☐ No, I need to work on this first.

3. Is my income stable and predictable month to month? Commission-only, gig income, or highly variable earnings make the surplus math harder to rely on.

☐ Yes, steady and predictable.

☐ It varies, I need to think about this.

4. Do I have a real monthly surplus — and have I actually verified it? Not what you think you spend. What you actually spend. If you haven't tracked it for at least a month, the number in your head is probably optimistic. Subtract real expenses from real take-home. What's left?

My estimated monthly surplus: $_____

Anything under $500 is thin. $1,500 or more is where this strategy starts to run well.

5. Am I planning to stay in this home for at least 2–3 years? The closing costs need time to recoup. Most people hit break-even between month 12 and month 18. If you're moving sooner, the math gets tight.

☐ Yes, I'm staying put.

☐ Uncertain, I should run the break-even first.

6. Can I handle a variable rate — honestly? If rates climbed 3 points, would your surplus survive it? Go back to Chapter 5 and run your own version of the stress test table. If a rate move would wipe out your gap entirely, you're not ready yet.

☐ Yes, I stress-tested it and I'm comfortable.

☐ I need to run that math first.

7. Will I treat available credit like a mortgage — not a spending account? Only you know the honest answer to this one. Talk to the person in your house who knows how the credit cards actually get used.

☐ Yes, I've thought about it and I'm confident.

☐ I need to have that conversation first.

8. Am I in Texas? Texas has specific constitutional rules around home equity lending. Not a dealbreaker — but the conversation starts differently. Call before you assume anything.

☐ No

☐ Yes, I'll call first.

So where do you land?

Mostly green? Real surplus, solid equity, stable income, and you're staying put — run your numbers. Go to **KeepTheCash.com/heloc-calculator** and see what your specific situation looks like. Then call.

Not quite there? That's not a no. That's a *not yet*. The math doesn't change. Your position does. Come back when the equity builds, the surplus strengthens, or the income steadies out. This strategy will still be here.

And if you're somewhere in the middle and you're not sure — that's what the conversation is for.

The Keep The Cash MORTGAGE Checklist

Step 1: Know What You Actually Earn and What You Actually Spend

Before you do anything else, sit down and be brutally honest with yourself about two numbers — your real monthly take-home and your real monthly expenses. Not what you think you spend. What you actually spend. Go pull the bank statements. I'll wait. The gap between those two numbers — that's your weapon. That's the whole strategy. If the gap is thin, the strategy slows down. If the gap is real, this thing runs. Your loan officer needs these two numbers before anything else, and so do you.

Step 2: Replace Your Mortgage with a First Lien HELOC

This is not a second mortgage. I need you to hear that. A First Lien HELOC *replaces* your existing mortgage entirely. It becomes the primary lien on your home — same house, same ownership, completely different financial engine underneath it. Your old mortgage gets paid off at closing. What you're left with is a line of credit that also works like a checking account. That's not a typo. That's the whole thing.

Step 3: Point Your Direct Deposit Here — Not to a Separate Bank

The second your HELOC is set up, your paycheck stops going to a regular checking account and starts landing directly in the HELOC. The moment that deposit hits, your outstanding balance drops. And because interest on a First Lien HELOC accrues daily on the actual balance — not on some fixed number the bank decided on the first of the month — a lower balance means less interest charged tomorrow. Automatically. Without you doing one more thing.

Step 4: Live Your Normal Life Out of the HELOC

Pay your groceries, your utilities, your car payment, your electric bill — all of it — straight from the HELOC account. You get a debit card. You get check writing. You get bill pay. It works like a checking account because it *is* a checking account. The difference is that the money sitting in it between when you earn it and when you spend it isn't just sitting there doing nothing. It's grinding down your balance every single day.

Step 5: Don't Draw the Balance Back Up

This is where people blow it. The equity you build is accessible — that's actually one of the best features of this thing — but drawing it back out every time the balance drops defeats the whole purpose. The strategy works because your surplus stays in the account and compounds against your debt. You want your average daily balance going down every month, not sideways. Spend what you need. Don't manufacture reasons to spend more just because you can see the available credit sitting there.

Step 6: Understand the Variable Rate — and Don't Panic About It

Yes, the rate adjusts. It's tied to SOFR and it moves with the market. I'm not going to pretend otherwise. But here's what most people miss when they hear "variable rate" and their stomach drops: the payoff speed of this strategy isn't primarily driven by the rate. It's driven by the gap between what you earn and what you spend. A three-point rate increase adds less than two years to your payoff timeline and you're still saving hundreds of thousands of dollars compared to finishing a 30-year mortgage. The rate is a headwind. It is not a wall.

Step 7: Run the Real Numbers with Someone Who's Not Selling You Something

Before you sign anything, get an honest look at your break-even timeline, your stress-tested payoff scenarios at different rate environments, and whether your surplus is real enough to make this work for your specific situation. If the numbers don't hold up, a straight-shooting loan officer tells you that before you spend a dime. If someone's showing you only best-case scenarios and moving fast, slow down. This strategy is powerful when it fits. It is not for everyone, and anyone telling you it's for everyone is the one you should walk away from.

> **The traditional mortgage is designed to slow your momentum down. The First Lien HELOC is designed to let it run. Those are two very different machines — and now you know which one you're driving.**

> **Ready to run your numbers? Go to KeepTheCash.com/heloc or call Michael Dendy directly at 615-499-6335.**

About Michael Dendy

I grew up in Marietta, Georgia. Southern born, southern bred — you know the rest.

I met Melissa in high school. She was fourteen. I was seventeen. I called her Bo somewhere along the way and it stuck. We got married in January of 1993, when I was 22 and she was 19, and we've been figuring it out together ever since. Thirty-three years and counting.

We have twelve kids. I'll let that land for a second. Twelve. Two grandkids now too, which means the table just keeps getting bigger. We've also got a dog named Kylo and a turtle named Tot, because apparently we don't believe in small households.

Before I ever touched a mortgage file, I was a pastor for seventeen years. Kitchen tables, hard conversations, people carrying weight they didn't know how to put down. That part of the job wasn't so different from this one. The math changed. The people didn't.

I became a mortgage loan officer because I needed to close loans. Twelve kids will do that to you. But somewhere in the middle of all those closings, I started seeing something I couldn't unsee. Good families doing everything right and handing hundreds of thousands of dollars to a bank because nobody ever showed them there was a different way. The door was always there. It just wasn't marked.

That's why I built Keep The Cash. And why I wrote this book.

I'm not writing it from the other side of a paid-off house. Bo and I are working our own strategy right now, same as you. I'm in this with you.

You can reach me directly at **615-499-6335** or **info@keepthecash.com**…I answer.

I HAVE 12 KIDS…I HAVE TO CLOSE LOANS!